Otherwise Occupied

Sally Ann Murray

Otherwise Occupied

Dryad Press (Pty) Ltd
Postnet Suite 281, Private Bag X16, Constantia, 7848, Cape Town, South Africa
www.dryadpress.co.za
business@dryadpress.co.za

Cover artwork: with thanks to Renée Rossouw
Kabuki in ochre, linocut on Zerkel Lithograph Paper, 687mm x 798mm,
Edition of 1, As part of 'Geon', a show at World Art, June 2018
Cover design and typography: Stephen Symons
Copyright © photograph of Sally Ann Murray: J Passerini
Editor: Michèle Betty
Copy Editor: Helena Janisch
Set in 9.5/14pt Palatino Linotype
Printed and bound by Digital Action (Pty) Ltd

First published in Cape Town, South Africa by Dryad Press, 2019

ISBN: 978-0-6399141-7-6

Otherwise Occupied

by

Sally Ann Murray

DRYAD PRESS

People! Read Poetry

Also by Sally Ann Murray

Small Moving Parts (Kwela, 2009)

open season (HardPressd, 2006)

Shifting (Carrefour Press, 1992)

CONTENTS

For A M-S and realising poetential

New Laid

In that bed a child's blanket
seems a simple cover. A quilt
she knows will take the time
it takes until a heart is bone
steeped soft in vinegar.

A skinned ribcage can be made
supple to bend like willow.

If only a bird, the bride imagines,
wing almost in hand,
airy feathers pillowing a bush.

now there was

once a nice girl
reduced to a minor character
in a life that took up
air though no space at all

so she left

and embracing
unexpected adventures
in empty arms she learnt
(as they say) a lot

one day

given a mirror's imperfect eye
she happened to stop
in a place people pass frequently
on their way to somewhere else

so now

at great length
I lie alongside you
beginning without starting over
as you turn to me

again

our gravities amo amas
amassing more or less as
bodies making room

homiletics

everyone lives his own happiness
her own misery or their vice versa

some men clubbing baby seals
is the other side of some women
cuddling babies in the scale of things

or some men cuddling baby seals
and some women clubbing babies

it depends on who you are
and who the other parties are
and what you're party to
and where the party is
and when and how involved

kin/d

in the day my frog face
never seemed to fit ok
mirrored in the lift

even nights were lonely sounds
killed with plugs that eared
the frog errors out but held
thoughts' water in until
a sleepless hollow head
sculled from jug to scalp

then slowly over jellied nights
the day face slipped
further and further down
and a tongue lying
against eye teeth flicked
from deep to extended reach

so frightened by becoming
I still killed the frogs—
even after I knew

Boundless

You have no boundaries, he always said.
It's true. The time for that has long gone.
Me, I keep coming back to the same
old questions that petals never answer
no matter how many times.

Love me. Love me not.
As I am, I am. Neither
here nor there.
Nothing to explain.

I don't know about borders.
They seem porous. It's always
the heart that gives.

You feel bound to weather
the tiny cuts that come and come.
It's for the best. Give it time.
You look for where the truth lies
in these words. Ashes. A hole.
Either way, you go home
and home is gone. So you mind
the extra mug. The dip in the bed.
The quiet voice gone missing.

Not Personal

Goats trample road verge death's head poster smiles
Votela ANC! A shopping trolley over-turned
among dumped paint tins and a junked fridge
inside which gap a man squats, head tipped.
Straightens. Exits. Stretches.
Extracts from tattered jacket
manicure scissors and in the brittle grass,
habit as a mirror, trims—*snip, snip, snip*—
his stubble barbered neat.
Then the deft reach
to nails—both hands and feet.

Does it matter that I see
without being intrusive?
Either way, surely it's conclusive:
such personal care performs a public
nota bene noting something
in the margins that is important?

Harbouring

Wharf swallows hard but chokes on corrugated
boxes and steelstacked yards—a needwide world.

Lost at sea, containers drop unfound. Hull
iceberg-like in lulling dip and rise and wait
till unrecovered hit or miss, the watertight
seals leak and boxes sink, bottoming out unseen.

Daylight broken in brings a dismembered stretch
of limited beach. Lids topless, disposable
plastic spoons, straws, tubes, terrific plastic lighters,
ceramic spark plugs, shopping bag skins and tin ugly tarnished
sinkers gather in waxy pellet polystyrene garnish.

None of which can hold a candle to the bloated
toby fish, body blown aghast to grotesque mask.

And down among the spine of dolosse knuckles
littered with dead sardine heads gilled and delicate neon lines,
a boy baits a hook, casts and sits. His book absorbs him into water.
Waiting for fish to feed, he reads: *How To Get The Love You Need.*

Risk being

second to none or nothing at all
looking for love from a haughty girl

she buckled, gave up. So ok, she admits:
though frisky, she lacked the appetite for risk.

Had no seat to back high horses
when iffy tempers might not run the courses.

But now, pride aside, would you give
a shit for missing love? I've

come to know that loving is not compulsory.
Your demons can be taught to live quite comfortably

at arm's length until you need them closer to the door.

no love lost

black dog snores absorb the gap
of silent food shovelled
without pause

curled ampersand dog warms
the bed that has turned
against them

in his sleep the man
reaches out to stroke
dog's head or woman's back

and some phantom leaves
a feeling like enough
to pass for love

morning on her neck reveals
a new dark mole fat tick
she picks it off

at the tender
bite and bleeding
fixes him with a look

nails the flailing body
to blood without
a second thought

It's only winter water

man so let's do this puppy—you are so slow dad; your great-grandmother
can do better and she's long gone; maybe you two share
a brain cell huh. Huh? Answer me!

(He's numb with cold, easing in, up to his ankles, up to his shins.)

I know Shakespeare also started as a baby but dad,
why you such a wuss, why must this take forever?
Like imagine, can you see, I'm married already?

(Ms Motor Mouth treads furious water between each diss.)

Now I've got two children.
Now they're at school.
Now they're teenagers.
Now they're grown up.
Now I'm getting old.
And now I'm dead, dad,
and you still not in the water!
Tell me how's this swimming gonna work?
Why'd I even put you in this story?

(Up to his neck now and overpowered,
his reluctance caves and ah cold, cold,
shrivelling cold in the water and she's latched,
a loving leech clamped on steroids
as they duck and dunk.)

Do this dad! Do that! Now watch me swim between your legs.

(Fails, comes up for air, gasps, yells…)

Open your gates you tool!

> (Slippery seals right through and back again
> and again and again
> and again and then
> that's done—so change of tactic.)

Move over there and stand still and close your legs
stupid and Watch Me Dad! Watch me demonstrate
the super woman power of the monster water wedgie!

Little Joys

Why gladhand to land the guy with the chiselled jaw
when afterwards you're bound for life to accommodate
his intensive grooming? You wait and see. He'll routinely
need the basin with the better light. The other mirror
will stand accused of foxing. The lotions potions Clooney
smoothers will take up vanity space end to end
and all to end, just the same, as fated.

Love's the culprit; cunning bait-and-switch.
Reliably, after n+ sexy dates, even the modern man
in one strong hand (choose L or R) must proffer
a velvet box, within which shiny crotch an itchy diamond knot.

Call me cynical. A bad-mouthed bitch not anyway feminine
enough for such ritual female gongs. I admit.
I have no appetite for the packaged to and fro;
the conventional ping and its inevitable partner,
the rebounding pong; I will never be voted Miss Congeniality;
am easily outstripped by the stiff competition;
the first and last time someone called me Baby was at birth.

But does that make me otherwise?
Flexibility is key. I can touch my toes and all the other
unladylike bits. Can do old-fashioned banana splits.
And while there's no open door policy, I offer
a fully-stocked mini bar well worth the tasting
should you crack the nod. Be my guest,
though I won't press.

Head askance, you cock my nearly hard
of hearing nonsense, nudging over

I budge, a little stiff to be honest,
but happy to be here undone,

unfinished promises coming to something
sometime—if slow to get going.

Life Support

shop cushions, covers & inners hello there printed tapestry printed digital family textured eyelet illustrated houses tweedle weave vintage royale triangle feather crewel Indian scatter jute geometric Jacobean rose fusion free inner printed scatter tartan tweed colonial previous classic stripe classic flowers botanical sundial African botanical printed Strelitzia printed Protea shaped cactus feminine botanical pastel script plain feather urban fringe forest birds colab tricam flamingo weave silk pouffe printed femme butterfly chenille Kensington butterfly breeze cut velvet chair pad taffeta geometric arrows printed wild life zebra slub tapestry kudu large Kuba printed zagora aurora scatter jacquard damask feather printed tribal lady cotton bobbles mock suede ethnic nguni velvet Grace Kelly French chateau embroidered cut garden woven diamond crochet printed moon on top Marilyn front and back Biko face Maasai lady microfiber Cuba size embossed small abstract appliqué lady Marrakesh piped retro Moroccan ethnic tassels colab tricam mendhi printed yarn dye lkboard keep it real words print inner blossom scroll b tapestry knit fish cal colour but button bedroll farm life ed artisan ne wash dog digital textured scotty ostrich printed painterly big buck tapestry house rules rope weave multicolour baroque flocking mock suede two tone floor hypo allergenic two pack crossroads load more living room 1 2 3 4 5 6 7 8 9 10 11 12 next no space. edit space? curate cushions closer? make selection? view cart? browse one-time sofa specials now?

Rubbish

After years as a reliable river, the water falls
low, stomaching cardboard chyme, scrap metal, a gutted sofa. All

kinds of plastic. Stalled, the flow knows no difference between stinks.
Near the sewage works, things float for a while, bloat, settle, sink

to sediment, silting the toll of sludge. Sometimes, city workers
move in with trucks to dredge and grade, dislodging junk from the murk

of Port Jackson willows banking on broken shade.
Near the roadworks sit the regulars, half-dressed, exposed for trade.

One woman picks out her Afro; sticks the comb behind her ear; adjusts her bra.
Traffic fumes in passing. Stop/go. A potential client idles up; cop exits car.

> *Sorry, that is such a rubbish poem, mom. It's not even*
> *a poem. It doesn't go anywhere. How dumb.*
>
> *(It's still rough. Not done! But it's about trying to*
> *make connections by...)*
>
> *Whatever. Please can we just kick it already. Ok? I've*
> *got a life. Places to go. And all this waiting for your*
> *writing. I'm like already really, really late.*

Body Works

A big woman lumbering
up stroke (and down hill)
breasts poems baggage
an unbecoming struggle
over thirty years
over forty years
over over oh for
neat cupfuls sweet couplets
over fifty over
what's next? *Oh! fuhgeddid!*
Sitting pretty might be a relief;
would allow an unobstructed
gently undulating view.

Instead, unruly handfuls
hands full, back strapped strapped back,
crossover underwired ironclad,
no place for irony
if you're mad enough
to risk skin-toned lycra.

Oh she longs and longs
for nothing; the next to nothing
of champagne glass perfection
of gnat tit numbies;
of sweet blow all.

But no, no. There's no
exchange, no guarantees.
These are hers to carry,
her burden to over shoulder

boulder holder baggy words
bigger shirts plus-size stretch
her shortcomings and her longings
embodied in body works
for the long trucking haul
of road works, detours, mounting kerbs,
mountain passes, passing valleys,
cupped ledges and some low-slung
hourglass curves… slow down
you over-hasty, you rough road hog,
you monster hauler. *Stop!*

Be careful. Go slowly.
There are necessary speed bumps,
there are truly moving mounds,
there are rare and beautiful
tortoises crossing on the road ahead.

Husband and Wife

Sometimes, the lonely care
is what they share the most:
solitary of connections;
a slow bind holding fast as the fact
of a bonded house tipped skew by roots
grown thick over years; the size
of dimpled thighs that still catch
in the throat of embrace.

Which is not to speak (mind you)
of some said woe that is in marriage
but to know about being
fitted for an unexpected brace
in place of a lonely body. Bones
carried so long by the length
of a flexing curve that legs have turned
into a shank of dependable rope.

In a pinch, this supple rope will do to winch
down (*slowly*) a concrete pot or, reaching tree to tree,
make shift a fine spring line for throwing over heavy washing.
Whatever the intended use, do keep this coil safely stowed.
For you too, with your braided cable, you two may also learn
to tie cast tow swing noose knot loop throw haul—
and (should it come to that) play tug of war
across an ailing rose bush, stuck with thorns.

Connections

A single hornet vectors the bedroom
struck from the vault between her thighs
volting across the current outage.

Vexed, the man in the kitchen hectors
a fruitless foraging. Hacks himself
a bludgeon of bread.

Upon a papery bed, the child's curled sleep
could pose the question: husk or pupa—
but who would know to ask?

Family House

Months on the market when a window of opportunity opens. The famous architect pays a visit, en famille. He narrow eyes our house declaring, *I would x and y and z*, an impromptu infrastructural aria flashy air-guitaring the domestic space without supporting beams. That's a maven for you. Maverick ideas are meant to hold their own in tension. We're just waiting for him to sign on the dotted line, now held in suspension.

But no, moving on and through (*fab view*) he suspects the house is only nice. Has too much shade. He shudders. Squints at the sun. Turns. Studies the sky. It's the sun. Always the damn sun. Then again, a wall can be demolished as easily as a woman's argument. *You should open up more* (turns to me). *Put a team on it. Less than an hour, this is gone. History. The trees? A pity but another easy job. One togt with a chainsaw. Single morning. That's that. Nothing to worry about. I'd sort this place out. Clean it up.*

This man is so amazing he comes once, twice, my god, *thrice* he comes to consider his options, being an intellectual of sorts, you see, a hands-on man who also has Many Significant Thoughts. Again striding up the garden steps, looking to the skies, raising his arms, describing a vast arc across the blue, willing the sun to move on demand. Behind him, again, again in step, step a pale wife and two small, obedient girls, all paying their careful dues.

The mother and daughters are mute and thin. They sit tight, stand holding hands, waiting out the surge and froth of the customary holding forth. Confidence creaming, he reminds us (again) of his Upper Case. *Because I designed the new pier and the and the and the the oh and btw House Rath? That's also mine. And don't talk to me about footprints*, he says. *I've reduced mine to nothing. Three solar geysers I put in. Three.* (His wife nods. The daughters nod, nod. Perhaps they feel for the numbers. Perhaps the wife is wondering whether ego and eco can ever reconcile.) Lithely up. Athletically down. Then two steps at a time heads up once more and downstairs ditto. Every move the darting eyes of the woman follow; the little girls shadow ducklings to her nerves. His voice rings in the stairwell, no number of footsteps or solid wooden floorboards able to drown him out. Announces: *Lekker possie this. Many worse places you could have grown up dude!* Our son gives him the blank, but that doesn't stick. Water off a duck's back.

I wait in a pool of quiet with his family in the lounge. The woman, the girls, peer cautiously into cabinets, a salvaged world of bone, rock, speckled eggs, beach glass and pottery shards. I barely hear her speak: *It's nice. All this.* (We smile.) *He hates stuff,* she murmurs. *Says he's got enough dust with three of us.* Himself suddenly appears. *S'not bad. Not quite historic but 'character'.* Turns deliberately through slow degrees, sketching space within his sphere. At the kitchen, his aura pauses. Expands. *Hnh! Looks like one of mine if you don't look too closely. My trademark simple style. And those: beautiful doors. First growth Oregon. Very unusual.* (I don't respond. Refuse the loaded compliments. Refuse to nod to god. This is still our home & we have lived here long & we have grown to love those doors with an affection opened in us by the daily opening of simply lovely doors.)

Ok team, he spins on his heels and claps his hands, *I'm done. Let's scoot.* He shooshes them out. *My people might be in touch*, he calls over his shoulder, a parting shot down the leafy garden flight. In his rippled wake the woman glances back. Gives half a waist-high wave. The little girl wings do the same.

same difference some difference

a mother reads the eddies
of her dauxghter's fluid

envies her the freedom
of a new girl's tender kiss

the secret life in the bathroom
barely a mirror outline condensed

yet also fears this pipe dreaming
body wanting to breathe underwater

while renouncing gills
girl leg propped struggles unsteady

the razored floor water wasting
unbalanced toward the plug

hoping that down under really is Australia
ready and waiting on the other side

Twelve/ Terrible/ Offcuts/

1
We all want the same thing, I promise.
Your happiness. Why grimace? I'm being honest.

2
Just hear me out:
I've asked nicely. Tried to help. Please don't… No, I will! Now I will shout!

3
You speak to me like—no, no, *you* shut up. *You*. For the last time don't cut
your pillows your duvet your desk your laces your space-case all your stuff.

4
You ruin everything. Your back-pack your books your expensive Vans
that brand new H & M shirt! Hell man

5
we only bought that, when? Two months ago? Old is *not* one season;
be reasonable! Rather let me give clothes to people who might need them.

6
Some poor kid would *love* what you trash. Think about it!
Instead you keep cutting. Jeans hoodies—this destructive habit—

7
boxers binders and if you didn't do that crazy behaviour you wouldn't have to hide
the evidence everywhere, which btw I always *find.*

8
You're struggling? Shit so am *I*. Razors sharpeners penknives blades you hoard.
It's like you don't know the obvious difference between what's bad and what's good

9

for you. All this constant rubbish, trashing, breaking. If this is your mind—
this mess—jesus. And now you're posting wild

10

intentions on Facebook or Instagram or whatever I don't know. *Why*? A bleeding cut
my child is not a suitable profile picture! What

11

are you thinking? Please, enough. I'm begging you. Look, I understand. I know you…
I know you cut the stuff to stop from what you'd otherwise do

12

and that is something. It's good. But still I just. I just don't know how to get through
to you my love my child. How to get my love through to you.

Constant Battles

Really? *Blah blah.* I'll give you blah blah.
I've also been young and even with new sleep science it's no
excuse for sleeping away the entire day and living like a pig you little *sloth.*

No, I said *sloth.* I did. I did not say *slut.* I didn't.
You deliberately misheard me. On purpose.
I'm not going to argue, just clean up this damn hole.

   It's my *room.*

Yes, it's your room, but it's our house, okay. *Ours.* All of us.
We all live here and pretty soon roaches and flies will be our closest relatives.
Plus, *plus,* since we're actually talking: I'm sick of washing *clean* clothes
that you're too lazy to hang up. There's a water shortage,
for pete's sake. That's why the short shower rule.
And while we're on that subject, can you tell me
why all these dirty mugs live in your room?
Crockery belongs in the kitchen. And these disgusting
tea bags stuck to the bottom?

        (She sees the ring stains
        on the desk. Intersecting sets
        and oddly pleasing orbits.)

And this? You've sharpened your pencils
on the bed! Among the bedding?

        (Grey lead and rainbow flecks.
        Orange. Violet. Yellow. Green.)

Is there any point explaining?
I use that for shading.
It's a special effect. *A technique.*

> (The mother studies the haunted portrait.
> Yet another young male face.
> Ghoulish colours. Hoodie.
> Hiding. Eyes hollowed gaunt.
> Who is she looking at?)

Shading? Well, that's no defence for dirt.
We all know your prodigious artistic talent but this...

> *My talent for messing up, you mean?*
> *That's what you mean, isn't it?*
> *Well my room is art.*
> *It's where I make*
> *myself me.*

> (Silence. Stand off. Stalemate.)

> *I don't know, mom. I guess. I just...*
> *the world is such a fucking mess*
> *such a mess. Do you even care?*

> *How can you worry about this*
> *a stupid bedroom when there's*
> *what's happening in Aleppo?*
> *Have you heard about that crisis?*

> (The mother nods.)

> *Mom, what is actually*
> *happening in Aleppo?*

(She sits down uninvited on the dump of
sheets & clothes & rags & cups & kak &
tries to explain about rebel strongholds &
government bombs & more than 4 years &
the Russians & then the Brits & _____)

But why's Britain involved?

(It's complicated.)

Right. So all of these people —

(Now there's a tiny picture of the evacuation
on the fone screen, truck after truck flanked
by cratered ruin. Gutted flats satellite dishes
streams of people a white flag waving —)

I don't understand, mom. I
honestly do not understand. Why
on earth is there always this fighting?
Why? Look! *There's mothers there.*
Dads. Little kids. Old women like
gran just trying to live their lives
like all of us. They're people. *We're*
related. It scares me, ma. That
somehow their distant hell could
be our country's close relation.

Do not deliberately

dwell on murdered girls but their keening cuts me, piercing any given day or night
a stranglehold a rape a rock to the head a knife a screwdriver.

The blunt force of obliterated lives knocks me down, each piecemeal news account
a breaking sadness impossible to reason or to bear.

Ohghostsohgodsohghosts who wander through Tokai Hlabisa Mitchells Plain
and Stellenbosch staggering across veld city farm forest

in hope of finding your rest in me where many buried girls live large. Another girl
jogging or coming from school or doing a good turn or going to buy milk for ouma

and suddenly *please help me pls hlp m help help* always I am too late too late
and they wake me in their shadows clawing calling me

awake until I am sodden with such a flood it cannot be only tears for all the endless girls
who never dry up. Girls ended again and again, calling out for ma

mommy mamie mummy mom mama as they die, desperate for some last trace of love;
flailing to escape the end of love, all love denied.

Their haunting lines my face, breaks my sleep, makes me live constantly at a loss,
palled with the lives of the girlish dead—a commonplace awful grief.

#redsky

When a sky spans red before the twinkling stars, a trick of light,
are there still somewhere shepherds sweet, innocently to delight?

And morning come, red slash fresh bleed,
would shepherds such as these feel some unease

for nights dragged darkly after dawn? Take a throated goat girl spread
on gargoyled haunches. How can she scan the skies for comfort, given what's red

and rising? They say it's common news a doe in heat will flag her tail often;
all does do. But answer me a truth, weighed and wanting: the day she knows the custom

course of violence, will she not buck unstruck to grasp
the fact that all your stars—though light years streaming—are fallen stars

already washed up
dead?

Holiday

He worked hard the whole year. This was his me time.
He'd caught crayfish. Caught them and cooked them. His family ate.

The teenage daughter, live streaming,
disappeared inside for days, a single cell organism.

Over the wall, my neighbour said she'd spent
the last month living under water.
Rough, she said, the sea's battering, but bliss.
Her face looked water raw in the absent wave.
Bright fishes flickering salt.

The son was still on holiday, along with his madcap quips and queries,
a métier that usually drove her mad. She missed his boyful ease.

Her own old mother, ever unflappable, had sat hours
on the dunes under a big petalled umbrella.

If she saw a very fat man, or a Euro-trash
number in stretch lace, her mother said nothing,
she said, but pulled a funny face.
Not unkind. Just marking the small
extent of her passing pleasure.

Date/d

During the war, my mother said,
without stockings smart girls
would draw the line
in fine black pen
all the way up
their pale bare legs—
such a fine carefully-drawn line
the only means they had
to their desired end.

Old Dog Woman

The last one leaves her a wide bed.
Bony feet. Cold air where long ago
a lover once curled against the thin
animal ridges of her spine.

Slow paws. Grey head. The new dog arrives upstairs. Call it that, or
heaven. Comfort without cortisone, among every stripe every colour.
The rain, if it rained, would be cats and dogs. Unbelievable, but true.
Heads in the clouds, the animals chew the fat of missing years, stretched
out like pools of lazy sun. Come dinner, they feast on air, which doesn't
taste bland, as you might think. The new dog wolfs it down, this filling
emptiness. The flyless sleeps. This nameless place is paradise.

So passes the first day,
old dog growing younger by the second.

Downstairs, where old dog is dead,
no one knows this. If they did,
you would be taken for a fool,
your credulity ridiculed.

(Some people think they
know everything about dogs
and about everything more
besides. They will do any
thing to break your spirit.)

But this dog love is here
with you to stay.

In time, perhaps
you will understand.

Below, old dog woman microwaves her unfinished mug
of cold morning coffee, as she does every afternoon.
When the timer pings, she feels surprise.
She goes to the window, holding the leash
because she's holding the leash. She looks out.
Stares at the garden gate. Tries not to cry.
She folds up the soft harness. Cries.

Now it seems so easy to die, yet here she is.
Still alive. Olive tree. Wild iris. Blushing bride.
Spider begonia. Grass aloe. Artillery cover.
People waiting at the bus stop always say
her garden is a picture. There is no one right now.

She walks to the bedroom. Looks at
the three-quarter bed that's always been
just right. She straightens the quilt
and plumps the pillow. She folds
the dog blanket neatly in the basket.
She goes back to the kitchen.
She warms the mug again.
The clock ticks loudly.

Tongues

My husband was born in Mexico.
English is not the language his mother raised him.

I was born and raised in Finland.
English is also not my mother.

I prefer to write as speaking
I have a bigger accent.

Funnily, he has nothing
though if you listen closely

you could maybe hear him. He rolls
his r's a very little when he says three

or throw or thrive. I love
that about him. It is subtle.

I can think no one casually
hears it excepting me.

Also I love that he never
says *gringo* or *sombrero*

even for making a joke to keep
my visiting family entertained.

There can be a lesson in there
somewhere? Or at least a story.

I have come to think that *why*
is always in front of every thought.

It is Spanish grammar. The thought is always
preceded by a question mark.

That seems right.
¿Why know only in the end
that you are asking?

Afterward

Some fool called marriage an epitaph in the end.
How little some people know. Sometimes, a table may serve
as well for laying out a body, as for spreading a feast,
and if you tame a hawk, well, it may be right to hope
the raptor will stay small, and yet prove fierce enough to do the job.
In the same vein that time leaves traces on each leaf, a pomegranate tree
may prove itself: dropping red-bellied baby fruits when the winds blow wild
and still, in time, come around to hang with jewels of plenty, more fruit
than you alone can eat. A lifetime is that full. So then you gift your neighbour,
and savour in kind return the home-baked cake which makes the warm exchange,
and sit quietly to watch the welcome birds tuck into crumbs and fruit, the tiny beetles
glowing green against the broken redness. And when it gets too much, because it will,
when all this busy life gets the better of you, you let yourself cry, and crying,
heart-blind, you let her silly little dog in maddened sweetness jump up,
up into your empty lap. And you allow her loving tongue to lick your cheeks,
to lavish your lonely face with all its missing kisses.

Brothers

They had no quarrel with distance. Years away; a Thai
delay, but today (in a Cape gale) he must fetch his brother. Drives
to the airport. Bypasses arrivals; is blown left into a flapp
ing wasteland of warehouses, hangars, strapped
freight. US diplomatic pouches hunkering down tar.
Customs: organograms of time & space to track the far
fetched relations of people & things. Not close, these two. Apart,
their bond stayed fraught, so waiting out these halts & gaps
seems apt. Stands in the unmarked line, hoping he's right.
Contorts to sign, pen tethered by string to the belt
of a bulky official. How not to rant. But need bids
obedience: go there come here go back. Tracking slip
produced and still no sign of his brother. Until at last, a meagre
gate, he pays R700 in handling fees and in return receives
a small cardboard box. And that's it. What's left. Ash.
Oh: also the passport wrapped in plastic, intact.
Yet, the little he's given, he might as well be holding air,
four corners of the earth collapsed into a nowhere
shroud but raging wind. Back home, his wife hears
the car, the garage door, study quietly unlocked.
She imagines he puts a small box on a shelf among books,
with here and there a whatnot that's been mailed from Bali
India Sudan Egypt Vietnam China the UAE.
Later, stirring a mug of tea, he mulls: *that Isipingo snap, the three of us
boys before we started school and became Major, Minor, Minimus.*
She nods. Such gusts drifts whirls. How no one, in the end,
can fix the time they get to spend.

Of Some Kind

Baboon comes loping savage the dark in.
The hunger moon of me barks back
on his behalf, biting off a chunk
of jagged cloud. Nothing between
us this scant night but teeth
and threat as thin ice spikes
our bones. Again the solitary
moan. Mountain rogue alone
leaves his stony cliff to forage
scraps that limits have forgotten.

Caracal saunters through gnarled vines
sways heavy from behind her strength
draws my eyes through cordoned rows,
unfolds me, haunches swinging rocky slopes
seconds split before padded feet sprint,
gathering spirits into shadow.
My ears turn tuft to twitch me fly
among the rough terrain as rooikat slips to air
breathless questions in the grass, untrapped for now.

Porcupine pricks attention with scattered leavings.
I see him solitary. Burrow. Bulb. Debark.
Rootling arums about. No rush to quill.
His clumsy clatter strikes me. As lonely.
Maybe it was his mate those wayward weeks
ago that trundled no return. There is no knowing
if she was she the carcass who never heard the car,
a shiver spill of spines, a brutal toss of pick-up-sticks,
my pen thorns quivered in a clear glass vase.

Turning

Winds rotor high on the hospital
hill. A chopper a chopper a chop
per sets skids, hovering down rackets
sound, sits urgently down to ground
on the big red H of vivid emergency.

Sweep down: dark
harbour cranes the sea
taut quay   slack quay
here pallets [] stacked []
cross-docked break
bulk ro-ro boxes
steel water rope cold
chaining a reefer load

there perishable frozen cargo
wet bulk dry bulk hub port
packed Panamax polyplastics

rough water waves, an outer
anchorage humps a split half
shell. It is, as ancient sailors tell,
the cracked turtle back
on which the earth bowl rests.

Scutes gleaming, a turtle claws
the beach, climbs. Slowly, fore
legs dig a sandy body pit; hind
legs a laying chamber. Scoops
and shovels, unslips each egg
an oval measure lipped into a

dip. Slowly coverdigs. Turtle-tracking
back and forth as if bedding down
her clutch when all that's left is to turn away
until next time. Ponderously she hulks

her bulk to foam
and slides into the sea.
Her eye glands tear.
Science avers this liquid
process serves to clear the salt.

Alternative Ending

Then there's the other version: the mermaid goes maelstrom. The waves messed her
up pretty badly; she'd been distracted. Hadn't reckoned on some lame Prince's sorry
shipwreck drowning saga but, then again, he was a handsome charmer with those
long legs and she was giving him a second passing glance when, *whack*, she was
dumped, left winded on a grungy little strip of beach. Flat on her back. If she'd had a
crack it would have been open to public viewing, all those gob-smacked dumbstruck
lumpen lubbers. Staring. Some of them truly awful, joking and *poking*.

No wonder she was enraged.

Of course, of course, about collateral
damage she would be sorry:
innocent children, kind women, good men
she would be something sorry for their loss
but in summoning her tidal strength
could spare no fine distinction.
She had to make it mean, the wave,
to leave no doubt about intention.

And so she did.

***

Funny how you think it's just a fishy story
fit for fearing children. Big mistake.
Some things take a while
but they come to pass.
Better believe the scale
of the wave to come.
The watersurge, the reach
a devastating inundation zone,
where busy life turns coral bone
and humans: hazardous waste.

Know that coastlines will jolt and slide;
earth shift on its brittle axis
blackening a day fractionally shorter
then each day shortr and shrtr still;

sun hours sliced smaller
and smaller till only our
indelible darkness moves
across the waters,
and nothing else.

And should you, glass darkly,
somehow survive, you will have
nothing by heart but the hopeless
scrap commanding what's been left.

That you Walk Away At Once
from the unknown.
Do not approach.
Step away immediately
people, then wait.

Soon after,

we are left behind and learn to cup hands in fragile alliance.
Each pool is amber eyes and drowned insects. We bend down.
Lick leaves. Pee in bottles for later. We fear it will get worse.

Tired, we make mistakes more often. A canal we saw for water—we
drank. Two children died. We left them oilily iridescent. Dead dragonflies.
Our girl is still here, though thin. Each morning I hold a pearled shell to the light.

My stream grows darker. Unsuitable for drinking. My skin is salty.
You lack the tongue to tell the measure of my change. And the sea is the sea
but deceiving. Once, the sea was the water we walked towards

believing an idea could float a boat. Now, wet ankles mark a deadline
and the smallest fish scales a gun to the head. No one has any news.
We don't need the news to know that this will end badly.

don't easy tiger me

no rainbow no paper no right no word
        you straights don't have to come out
of any holes you just stay yourselves
        like yourself like you're already yourself
but for some of us a straight space is deadly
        and being among gays can be a bulls-eye
because even where queers are almost
        as common as regular raindrops some
people are still locked out
        and that is bullshit in a china shop
and whatever eventually happens
        you better believe I said it

we are not a disorder won't fall down broken
        by some old-fashioned logic
your fucking destructive defective thinking
        about us being damaged goods
responsible for your wasted breakage

He Reverses the Bathroom Ruling

People are making such a fuss about nothing.
If I saw a tranny in the men's he'd be a man so I wouldn't mind.

> Well, dad, she's not necessarily male identifying;
> she might be female identifying. And don't say tranny.

Sorry. 'Transvestite'. Is that what the ladies like to be called?

> No! That's so '70s. Show some respect. *Transgender.*
> Or transman. Or transwoman. Though really
> the word should just be 'woman' or 'man'.

I understand maybe it's safety or privacy but doesn't it seem wrong to make them a
special toilet category, to make them even more different than they already are?

> Them? Who's that? Would you want to be 'them'?

Well, sorry, I don't want to be them, god knows I don't. (Humpfs.) But shouldn't the
rest of us adjust? Here's my thinking:

if a transman uses the men's   *if a transwoman uses the women's*
it's because he's a man   *it's because she's a woman*
the other men must change   *the other women must change*
their thinking   *their thinking*

Wouldn't that solve the problem?

> Dad!

What, what now? Oh! No, rather, I mean, 'when' a transman, or a transwoman. Not
'if'. And is it the other way around? The woman first, not the man?

Are you doing this on purpose? Are you deliberately
making this hard for anyone to follow?

Am I... what? No!

Dad   it's   not   that   difficult!
Even for you. A cis-gendered heteropatriarchal guy
but still probably quite intelligent.

Well, I do want to be understanding otherwise...

Oh, excuse me Sir! So *generous*!

No I'm not looking to be offensive; I just want to understand. And I am trying.

That's for sure. You are, *dad*.
Extremely fucking trying.

(tbc)

Former Child Star

I grew up in Cali. We didn't really have weather. Just sun.
My finest hour was when I turned sixteen only I didn't know it then.
There were the interviews, the crowds, the almost Oscar.

But people are cruel. They scorned my future.
I made some good films after, though not the sexy I got famous for.
I couldn't do it again and again. I'd had enough of pretending.

After the last disappointment, I was ready to disappear
and there was this Swedish director I'd worked with.
Critics said he'd had one hit too few; one mistress too many,

but he was rich and I was hot and we just tied the knot;
moved to Stockholm where everything is weather and even the short
days feel too long and too far away to be anything remotely

like California. Here's nice enough. Many islands. Many bridges.
If you want to visit, *Lonely Planet* is useful. Lists the Top Experiences:
Historiska museet, ABBA museet, Moderna museet.

Hagaparken. Thielska Galleriet. Everything. I would very much like to
do all that. Hop-on-hop-off I imagine would be interesting but my
husband does not enjoy crowds. He prefers just us, or himself.

Mostly, we watch my husband's films in the home surround cinema.
Calamitous Arrival? *A Woman Undone*? You may have seen these? In winter,
we burn his rivals' features onto discs; feed them to the fire.

My husband has an electronic weather station mounted on the wall.
His birthday gift to himself for reaching seventy. He monitors pressure,
wind speed, temperature. He likes to know exactly what is going on.

At our summerhouse, the airconditioning is high end. My husband
does not approve of climate. He prefers climate control. In the living room,
a picture window looks out along the Baltic coast. I can see storms

blow in suddenly. If it's bad, I stay inside and wash my hair upstairs
then maybe go downstairs and stay inside, for there's no real going out.
If he needs me, if he calls, I must be here. When he comes home,

he stands for long minutes at the window, whiskey glass in hand.
Usually it is already gloomy, but I think he likes to imagine he can see
what's coming in the clouds. For now, that is what I will let him believe.

Eventually, after the ICU,

he comes to, complains of black eggs breeding in his gut that filthy shit
the sheets. Damns the catheter, which is tubing macaroni into him long
after the pot is feeling bottled. He is so sick of these foreign bodies
bursting his bladder. *You mark my words,* his voice sidles, *these
nursing ones are sly sisters. They thieve a man's life!* He says they steal
his milk like dry old cows, fingers rubbing. *You wretched women,
watch out!* he shouts, grabbing the matron's closest arm other hand
cupping his crotch beneath the sheet. *I'm all here. Here's my tackle. I'm
not past it! I've still got all my kit.* At that, they push us out politely in
order to push him down. The last I see of him is the curved end of the
bed and ten featherless baby birds with horn-nailed beaks.

Lady Gaga's Super Bowl Performance Divides America

Shoutout to Lady Gaga's stomach roll for showing girls
that you don't need to have a perfect body to absolutely kill it;

love how Lady Gaga's belly bag over her shorts
makes her seem more relatable;

what I love most about @ladygaga's #SuperBowl halftime show —
her belly. Even if you have abs, real bodies have rolls when they move;

the fact that @ladygaga is out here performing in a belly shirt
without a flat & toned tummy & looks bomb, inspires me;

seeing Lady Gaga perform with a little fat on her belly
was the most inspirational thing of 2017;

frat daddies at this super bowl watch party just said Lady Gaga
had a belly and if she's got a belly then I'm concerned I'm obese;

bless Lady Gaga and her teeny tiny belly...
Normal girls RULE!;

Lady Gaga's belly is beautiful. Don't fatshame her.
(For girls who love warm bread and olive oil);

guys making fun of Lady Gaga's 'muffin top' is the reason
why girls have so many body image issues;

oh haters, how bad you must feel about yourself to bother with @ladygaga's
belly. Go have an ice cream cone and find some fucking joy;

stepdad @ladygaga *ew look at her belly fat, what a pig.*
Like, wowowow, women are not here for your validation!

@ladygaga belly jiggle during her performance
is the level of confidence I want to have;

people are actually talking shit about Lady Gaga's belly
like okay I fkn wish my belly looked like Lady Gaga's;

Lady Gaga might have a belly roll but she's got more
bank rolls than all you judgmental buttholes;

the best thing about the #PepsiHalftime was when my dad
said that Lady Gaga had a belly and my mom finally said he was a fucking idiot.

Empathy

Classic A-type personality. High achiever from young age. Always aced everything. By 33: string of first-class degrees behind her name. Award-winning monograph. Thriving psychiatric practice. Happy marriage. Achievements keep growing. No signs of slowing.

Her perfectly healthy pregnancy ends when she (is) delivered (of) stillborn twins. Dead baby boys so terribly exited of her empty body her sudden hollow. She gone gone gone time died of her she self loss what   what   what   is left.

She dreamed of looking for her lost babies as if she'd forgotten, in an absent-minded moment, where she'd left her passport, or her keys, or her heart. She left her husband, his kindness unbearable. Said nothing to anyone, many terrible things to herself.

Friends said the obvious: she'd lost her mind. Textbook study in falling apart. There were indeed long bouts of mania as she turned life away and grew the grief pinned to her shadow. Unfeeling wasps burrowed under her skin. She wrote everywhere, up and down her arm. (The arm, in medical parlance, being an extremity.)

She was followed by stray animals, mewling whining howling; was unable to look at life for fear of seeing death. She cried at flowers sun cars birds tomatoes paper keys couples shoes carpets toys babies. Liver made her cry. She cried when drawn to the sharp end of what a knife might mean, if she could let it. She could not stop crying trying to drain grief.

(& &)   her first tattoo

(&) (&)   her second

As the seasons turned to spring, she staked her pain, training a wall she held herself together with taut wires and cable ties, pinched buds recovering something of herself in layers, began to work again.

Patients found her both helpful and helpless. She understood their green ghosts. She knew them. That if skin held a body in, it also held true that bodies cannot withhold leakage. She sent her patients home with votives inked on tissues.

She has been better, true. But she has learned to keep absent company. Adopted a scruffy dog that destroys shoes and rugs and reason. The dog is a risk she is willing to take with her. Her research is coming along well, though some quibble at her minor interests:

- tentative thoughts on empathic pain as a double-edged sword; whether you hate emotion or love emotion;

- the way mascara, when a stage actress cries during a moving scene, runs from her left eye more quickly than her right.

If you ask Dr A, she will patiently explain: the right brain, which controls the opposite side of the body, also controls negative emotions. Therefore one side seems, and is, sadder than the other.

Genealogy for Girls

Everyone knows his first child
arrived in a box of instant fame later adding
a tween model with (also) two smash hits.
She and her famous father have not
gone public on who her mother is—
though we suspect it must be someone
impossibly pretty who could possibly
be either still alive, or sadly, now dead.

('What's on Kim Kardashian's feet?')

We're stanning his stunning second girl—
also incredibly gorgeous gifted talented
model daughter actress movie star
best-dressed television personality—
an influencer whose side-hustle face
crowd-funded her big mood beauty line.

('J-Lo flashes pink bra in see-thru shirt!')

His third daughter keeps it trill as a fashion
designer, author, brand ambassador
for an exclusive clothing line
(plus her latest venture an adorable
video for her new signature perfume).
She began life as an unknown reality star
and Wow! Look at her now! Killing it!

('Taylor Swift rocks a pair of short-shorts!')

His last daughter (to date) is total finesse.
With the most iconic look
and ten brand deals wrapped!
Every woman wants to be her!
So extra, she's made a name with her unique
aesthetic as international SUPERmodel.
It's easy to forget who her father is—
the girl could easily outshine him
and herself in the near future!

('*5 exercises women must stop doing now!*')

Adulting this narrative,
we can only hope that all four woke girls
don't let themselves go but prove
ageless, like their ever-handsome dad.

Darwin's Deliberations

(Second note. July 1838—date conjectural)

This is the question (circled, in pencil. Entire text written in pencil)

Marry	Not marry
Children (if it Please God)—Constant companion (& friend in old age) who will feel interested in one—object to be beloved & played with— —better than a dog anyhow—Home, & someone to take care of house—Charms of music & female chit-chat—These things good for one's health—*but terrible loss of time*—My God, it is intolerable to think of spending one's whole life, like a neuter bee, working, working, and nothing after all—No no won't do—Imagine living all one's day solitary in smoky dirty London House— Only picture to yourself a nice soft wife on a sofa with good fire, & books & music, perhaps—Compare this vision with the dingy reality of Grt. Marlbro' Street, London Marry—Marry—Marry Q.E.D	Freedom to go where one liked—Choice of Society & *little of it*—Conversation of clever men at clubs—Not forced to visit relatives & to bend in every trifle—to have the expense & anxiety of children— perhaps quarrelling—Loss of time— Cannot read in the evenings—Fatness and idleness—Anxiety & responsibility—Less money for books etc—If many children, forced to gain one's bread (But then it is very bad for one's health to work too much)—Perhaps my wife won't like London; then the sentence is banishment and degradation into indolent, idle fool It being proved necessary to Marry When? Soon or Late* —soon for otherwise bad—But then if I married tomorrow—an infinity of trouble & expense—fighting—awkwardness—poor slave—you will be worse than a negro— Never mind, trust to chance—keep a sharp look out—There is many a happy slave—

* Heading and subsequent text written on the *verso* of CD's note on marriage

Incredible But True! Phoenomenon

(Deponents)
further severally say that during the time they were present
said female appeared at one time very morose
and sullen, and retired into the little recess off the stage
and appeared unwilling to come out again when called by the Exhibitor
and the Exhibitor felt it necessary on that occasion to let down a curtain
and this, when drawn, separates the stage
and the little recess from the other part of this room
and the Exhibitor after the curtain was let down looked behind it
and shook his hand at her but without speaking
and he soon after drew up the Curtain
and again called her to public view
and she came again forward on the stage

(Sight-seers)
In the neighbourhood of London we found her surrounded by many persons, some
females among. One pinched her; one *gentleman* poked her with his cane; one *lady*
employed her parasol to ascertain that all was, as she called it, *nattral*. This inhuman
baiting the poor creature bore with sullen indifference, except upon some provocation,
when she seemed inclined to resent brutality. On these occasions it took all the
authority of the keeper to subdue her resentment.

Parties of Twelve and upwards, may be
accommodated with a Private Exhibition
at No. 225 Piccadilly, between Seven and
Eight o'Clock in the Evening, by giving
notice to the Door-Keeper the Day
previous. A woman will attend (should
she be so required).

(Henry Cesars)

To observe as a showman, I pray you:
has she not as good a right to exhibit herself
as an Irish Giant or a natural dwarf? She may
indeed give no reply, but please you enquire
of that man, by role her personal keeper,
to whom she has of own choice contracted.

       (Sara Baartman)

       Without coercion you give me liberty to say
       whether I am exhibited by my own consent?
       Through this my superfluous interpreter:
       I speak fluent English and Dutch.
       After Paris, I speak some French.
       I have not spoken Gonaquasub Khoe
       for many a year. Were I to speak as I spoke then,
       you would understand me even less.
       Had I always spoken as you always urged,
       understanding would be further faltered.
       Just know: I understand perfectly
       the tenses of your history though
       I would ask that also you comprehend
       why the extent of the understanding
       I extend you is of necessity slender.

       I have not spoken of this before. I speak now.
       If I have come here of my free will I came the same
       from the Cape of Good Hope after employment as a washer
       woman and a wet-nurse, with him here, Henry Cesars,
       he eager to leave for being increasingly in debt for his
       unfree status as a free black, the related unhappy lending
       terms extended him making life impossible to live
       and showmanship attractive. With the signed permission
       of Lord Caledon, Governor of the Cape, we embarked;
       came arranged to St James by the man Alexander Dunlop
       on the promise of shared profit from the Egyptian Hall

of Piccadilly Circus, and similar. If I came here, it was for no better
reason being that I stay there. Though I have come to perceive that
my willingness expressed, alleged by me in writ, is yet a feint. Coaxed
and bound despite my firm refusal to appear naked or permit
examination, I am bound always to be beholden. As for what
is to come, of that I cannot definitively speak except that I will
venture to speak of it, imagined, and still be speaking
when this said inquiry be done.

(Showman)
Subsequent to the event, we extend an Invitation to Witness! Also! The Spotted Boy, the
elegant dwarf (Count Boruwalski), the Living Skeleton DANIEL LAMBERT (50 stone
700 lb/317 kg), the Sicilian Fairy, a young lady measuring just 22½ inches tall), *et alii* living
curiosities.

(Scholar)
Rapidly following the Sara Baartman suit (1810), the list includes but is not limited to:
Sámi ('Laplanders' 1822) South Americans (1822) Esquimaux (*c.* 1820s) Native
Americans (1840s) San ('Bushmen' 1847) 'Aztecs' (1853) African 'Earthmen' (1853)
and of course the world famous troupe of authentic tribal warrior savage Afric Zulus
(1853) etcetera.

(Archive)
Let the records show that: in December 1811, Sarah Bartmann a female Hottentot from
the Colony of the Cape of Good Hope, born on the Borders of Caffaria, was baptised this
 Day *at Manchester Cathedral* by permission of the Lord Bishop of Chester in a letter
from his Lordship to Jos. Brookes Chaplain.

(extract)

Also in 1948

19 Nvmbr 1948
before
an audience of
dozen

two   neurosurgeons
than   neurologists
more   & psychiatrists
the 2 most   en thusia
stic and pro   lific lobot
omists in th   e Wester
n world fac   ed off aga
inst each ot   her in the t
heater at th   e Institute
of Living

each   man   had   his   single   turn   on   stage

First up: Professor William Beecher Scoville (Neuro surgery, Yale). His patient (*anon.*) conscious. The ad ministration of a local allowed surgeon to slice thro ugh the scalp and peel down the skin from the patie nt's forehead, exposing her skull. Quick work with a drill opened two holes, one over each eye. Now Scov ille could see her frontal lobes. He levered each side up with a flat blade so that he could perform what h e called 'orbital undercutting'. What followed was n ot quite cutting: instead Scoville inserted a suction c atheter—a small electrical vacuum cleaner—and suc ked out a portion of the patient's lobes. This patient was wheeled away; a replacement secured to the tab le.

Next: Walter Freeman, Professor of Neurology, George Washington University. He had no surgi cal training; no Connecticut medical licence. Fre eman's goal—an assembly-line approach. Lobot omy quickly and easily dispatched. His techniqu e allowed him to perform twenty-plus operation s in a single day. He proceeded to use shocks fro m an Electro-Convulsive Therapy machine to re nder his female patient unconscious, then insert ed an ice pick beneath the eyelid until the point rested on the thin bony orbit and a few quick hh hammer taps broke through the bone and allow ed him to sever portions of the frontal lobes via a sweeping motion of the pick. The instrument w as withdrawn and inserted into the other orbit, a nd within minutes, the process was over. Freema n boasted: an operation so simple he could teach any fool, (layman or psychiatrist), to perform it in all of twenty short minutes, give or take—

(Fate of both patients: unrecorded.)

Bonus Fun Facts!

Tens of thousands of lobotomies were performed in the US from 1936 onwards.

Well into the 1950s, major medical centres at Harvard, Yale, Columbia, and the University of Pennsylvania regularly improvised on Freeman's operation.

Your basic lobotomy involved drilling through the skull and, sight unseen, severing portions of the frontal lobes with an instrument (now obsolete) shaped like a butter knife. This procedure was known as a precision lobotomy.

Lobotomy's inventor, the Portuguese neurologist Egas Moniz, received the Nobel Prize in Medicine for his pains in 1949.

Mine and Others

He worked at the mine since two thousand six.
I went there after we got married. I was seventeen.
I was expecting the advertised life. Instead I was surprised.

The peaches in the front are for the neighbours.
The peaches at the back are for the family.
This year, both sides the crop is small.

He had a sweet tooth for tinned peaches.
That time, the police went door to door
breaking into homes, arresting miners
who had not gone to the mountain.

There were three hippos at the supermarket in town.
I didn't understand these men wearing balaclavas
and standing on the hippos all the time.
Afterwards, they said No, I had to wait until the mine got there.
The body wasn't mine. They told me to choose a coffin

although there was no budget for a funeral
because they didn't know people would die
so I was just on my own with the children.
The government came and said I must sign
for R15 000 funeral money but it would come later.
First I refused to sign. I have never seen the money.
The reason being, they say my husband was a criminal. That is why.
They tell me I must stop being a nuisance in this country.
They say I mustn't bring my ways this side, freeloading for parcels.
I must join the vegetable gardening, the sewing schemes.
I must keep busy. I know it is no good waiting. I don't wait.
The president doesn't come. And even if the president came.
Still, I think Mandela would have come to us.

All I do is think, think, and think.
I cannot find a job. If I go and find a job
then the children will have no one to cry to.
I feel sorry for my children because they look like orphans.
We have six South African children.
We were married twenty-five years.
He loved Rambo films. Ringo Madlongozi and Sotho music.
His big passion was Kaizer Chiefs.

My husband was one of those crazy ones
always shouting at the television and calling the referee a moegoe.
The dreams he had I hope to continue.
But I have no papers. To stay legal I must go every month to Lesotho
to get my passport stamped. The taxi costs R340.
With no papers it is also more difficult now.
Post Bank is going to close the family account
because they saw I am not a permanent resident.
They have given me three months' notice.

I am worried
what will happen
to the second payment
if it comes from Lonmin;
where it will go
without an account
in my name.

Slow Violence

Topics covered include
(but are not limited to)
time, water, shit, waste, academia,
labour, the school, the prison, the hospital,
mothers, fathers, teachers, dogs,
horses, locusts, boys, girls,
childhood, whiteness, blackness,
religion, rugby, language,
the category, the canon, the colony,
the beach, the woods, the city,
the dump site, the valley,
joy, melancholy, intimacy,
risk, death, danger, desire,

Sample Questions for a Senatorial Quorum

Is a human body in cold storage still a warm-blooded animal?
Could
his pink shirt cite intestinal flora in the *Journal of Gastroenterology*?
How
is it of consequence that the chief operational officer's curtains are well hung?
Will
the portfolio in blended learning finally align with his ability to minimise a window?
In
the debate around cultural authenticity, could her pearls really be real?
If
this collective body passes a motion, will it mean a messy end?
Are
there any more centenary cupcakes for a sugar rush towards the finish?

Skyromancescope

A woman finds a page packed
tight with drifting flakes blinking,
though her life cannot sow snow.
Banks of that she'll never know.

Here, her life, now seems the only
possible sky. No other unless
the mind's eye decides to launch
and make another orbit.

The world turning as it does, she paged
and landed on a man's memory
of a boy: a roof; a Russian

        exiled writer recalling
        how as a child he'd skipped mama's famous
        borscht to shiver on the black tarpaper
        skyjack of their housing block,
        lit windows winnowing
        the night of familiar faces.

        How hungry he'd been
        to spot a cosmic track
        blur and trace the future
        Vostok 1 Юрий Алексе́евич Гага́рин
        Polkovnik Gagarin. Hoping to see
        a single arcing of the earth,
        the hero circled and the boy
        saw all around him suddenly
        a shower of starry snow
        the milky way come raining down

each snowflake gone the instant it hit
and in a mad wish he flung himself, leapt
air bare where where and stunned
a breathless angel bodied in what should have
been the snow below. Came to with snowy stars,
and voices, his mother at the kitchen window,
shouting at him to *Come Right Now! Come now and eat!*
And he was hungry after all and up he got and went
and never said a word to anyone of his
boyhood madness. Till now. (*Sorry mama*. Bashfully,
he holds up a copy of his book, which is said to be a
pacy thriller about the space race.
But also, he says, a story of another life in me.)

Finding I's Inside Library Books

A mini wholewheat wrap, pressed like a flower
        (I felt peckish.
        Then the book got interesting.)

Ultrasound images of a foetus
        (I could not bear it.
        I hid them after I lost the baby.)

A letter in a sealed, stamped envelope
        (I was glad to know, after all those years.
        Thank you. Though it still hurts.)

Divorce papers
        (I didn't need them, as it happens. He died.
        I was the sole beneficiary.)

Laminated weed
        (I smoked, yes. And I also made bookmarks.
        Loved that stuff.)

R50
        (I got the book from my gran as a present.
        I hate books. I just gave it away.)

A used lottery ticket
        (I was always a loser, my wife said. Though I did try.
        Just out of interest: was the ticket by any chance in
        Your Essential Guide to Debt-Free Living?)

A cryptic note

(I wrote that note very clear, actually: It's Hard Imploring a
Donkey. They Hit Everything. My Only Neighbour Envies You.
Never Open Water With Heat Around Torches. Get it? Same code as
always. I was counting on my partner to get it. I even wrote: write
me back in the book, *Reusing Old Graves*, by Douglas Davies. Plain
and simple. I heard nothing. At first I thought my partner had
fallen off the wagon again, and forgot how to read, so drunk he
couldn't figure out my message. *I HID THE MONEY. NOW WHAT?*
What else could it be, that he didn't respond? I was basically
shouting it in his face same as whispering in his ear.

A month goes by and I'm on tender hooks or what, waiting for him
to make contact and bam! There's the exact book staring at me
from my wife's nightstand. She's checked the cursed Davies book out
the local library; renewed it once already, by the stamp. Sure, I knew
she had a liking for graves, which is maybe why I thought of that
book in the first place, but this? And happens she's a slow
reader. Not in that sense, just she extracts her enjoyment; likes to
savour. Otherwise what's the point? she says. I wanted to show her
what's the damn point right then and there! The pain I'm in. The
pleasure she's taking! So I'm waiting weeks for a reply but in the
meantime the book is bang under my nose out of circulation. I
coulda killed her. But of course not. She wasn't in on it; she had no
clue about the jobs I worked on the side, though honestly it was for
her, every time. Well, us. We needed the cash pretty bad. I won't go
into that, if you don't mind. Respect my privacy.

Though the story doesn't get better, neither. I wait. I want to make
sure it's safe to get the stash but also I'm worried Rick's thinking
I've stabbed him in the back and he's like to come after me. I'm
tense. So at the time I don't know why I don't hear from Rick but
now I know it's because the book's out so Rick hasn't heard from
me and then I hear on the radio a small-time crook name of Rich

Riley's been shot, killed in some bank job that evidently he didn't invite me on for lack of trust now, in view of the failed note.

So after a while with Rick dead I feel it's gone quiet and no one's any the wiser about me. I figure it's safe to get the stash, 'specially seeing as it's me wrote the note and only me got the note and that cash in effect now has my name writ on it. And whaddya know: money's gone. Nada. Some lucky buster's hit the jackpot and that sure weren't me. It never would be, either. That was it for me. Never robbed another cent, nor opened another book neither. Can you blame me? Not that I was a big reader before, as it happens. My wife's the reader of us. So these days the reading's on her side, same as ever. But it may be that a book's proven useful to us, despite, for as it's kept me an honest Joe these many years. At least that's something to be said for books, if nothing else.)

Re: Reading and Re-reading. Page Proofs

I

Reading aloud is much louder
than reading to yourself.
There is no wide ear
in the world likely to cup you
any comfort. So be prepared

for the sounds your voice will make
sine waves in the noises qua non
that do not allow you
to hear yourself speak.

For all the many years
of our marriage he has read
aloud to me for pleasure.

Various things. Whatever
he knows we might like
or need. What the times
require or what takes his fancy.

My husband, you understand,
he is definitely a certain type
of man who can tell you
a thing or two about many things
and he does tell things to many people
maybe even he will tell you something.
But when he reads aloud
he is different from himself.
Quiet. His reading expresses him.

His way to say the words of so many
other people, this reassures me.

Even when his readings
do not quite fit—
when they fill me
with the emptiness
of the world—
I like it.

When he reads aloud we are alive. We come alive.
He is alive or he wouldn't be reading to me.
When he stops reading to me
it will have happened,
it could happen then,
I will come to an end.

I hear the bones. His voice grows brittle.
On the spine so much hinges on his reading.
Reading can open, and reading can close.
I worry what will happen to the reading
of me when he no longer reads to me.

II

Many people do not read
even if they are world leaders.

You can probably think
of at least one big name

though he would not be ashamed.
He would say he is too busy

and that actually he does read
occasionally, a headline or two,
a tweet. Even a paragraph, perhaps,
if he is not too busy.
Because a man does not
become precedent by reading.
That would take too long.
Sad. Just sad.

Better to use the efficiency method:
common sense + knowledge =
correct decision [zero reading]

So that is proof.
Without reading
a president can come
to the correct decision.

But look lady, make no mistake,
I do read. I read passages,
I read areas, parts of chapters,
typical standard wall designs
as and when necessary.
I connect with the people.
I watch cable news. I tweet.
Often I am so busy I cannot read
even important documents.
I have people for that.
My designated people.

Books? Books are plain bad.
Most books are too long.
Fact. Ask anyone.
It's a tremendous problem.
Nothing can make books great again.

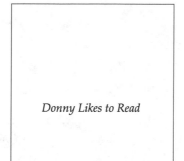

Donny Likes to Read

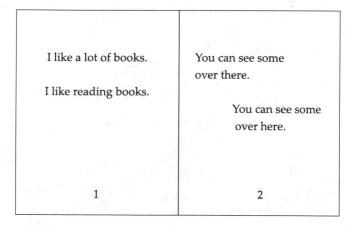

I like a lot of books.

I like reading books.

1

You can see some
over there.

You can see some
over here.

2

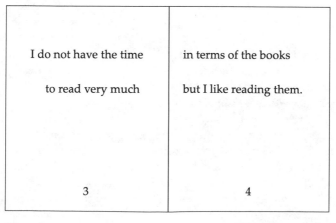

I do not have the time

to read very much

3

in terms of the books

but I like reading them.

4

Good reader = good governance? Joke!
At least read the Constitution.
More worrying things than this chump's bookshelf?

Like pussies, for example. Littitchurr is only for pussies. Though Potus
oh he does like pussies as much as that other pussy Potus liked books.
This present Potus does do pussies. Pussies are all for (this) Potus. There
should be a wet T-shirt for that. A series. Monday through Sunday.

PUSSIES FOR POTUS   FOR POTUS PUSSIES   PUSSIES ALL FOR P
    POTUS IS PUSSIES   4 FALL FOR POTUS   POT US SIES FOR PUS
    FOR POT US PUSSIES

I'm not sure how to read that.
I will read it any way I like.
I will then tell you how to read it
and you will read it as I told you.
Believe me, I know what I'm talking about.

III

Read My Top Pussy Pull Quotes

*I'd look at her right in that fat, ugly face of hers, I'd say you're fired. She is
unattractive, both inside and out. I fully understand why her former husband left her
for a man—he made a good decision. She cheated on him like a dog and will do it
again—just watch. He can do much better! If she can't satisfy her husband what
makes her think she can satisfy America? Sadly, she's no longer a 10. As long as
you've got a young and beautiful piece of ass, who wouldn't take her picture and
make lots of money if she does the nude sunbathing thing? And when you're a star
they let you do it. You can do anything. Whatever you want. Grab them by the pussy.
If she weren't my daughter, perhaps I'd be dating her. All of the women... all of them
flirted with me—consciously or unconsciously. That's to be expected. I was going to
hit her with her husband's women and I decided I shouldn't do it because her
daughter was in the room. That's my ethics talking. Anyway, well, at 12, I wasn't
interested. I've never been into that... but she was beautiful and I am probably going
to be dating her in ten years. Can you believe it? You'd fuck her, wouldn't you? C'mon,
wouldn't you?*

IV

Millions of people do read
but not in English.

I do not know what they are reading.
I can only imagine.

V

Once I was at a train
station in Bratislava, stranded.

I had to find a way
to get to The Castle on time
for dinner (The Dinner)

but the timetabled script was a mystery and I could not
make anything out. Whence or whither or wither
when a weird wildworn man stepped out
from behind a wheeled stand of old books,
one ragged as the next. He read
the fellow traveller in me,
offered feverishly to guide.

I was at a loss with the sound
of him, his odd English in my ears
but nor was I at liberty to refuse
whatever he was offering.
Which was help. I hoped.
I had no choice, I felt,
but to accept and go along.
Together (that's how it came to seem)
between us, he helped me read the signs.
He pointed: curled white words lettered
on the raised board. I tried to follow.

Братислав
Bojnicky zamok.

It was impossible my tongueyes
had disappeared choking closed
on no sense on non sense words
that meant something to him
and millions of others.

As I eventually understood him,
there was no train.
There never would be
another train. No train
anymore, not. Not to
where my train needed
me now to (soon to) go.

Suddenly he seemed sad for me.
Then went almost mad.
Grabbed my hand like a man
about to be abandoned. Pulled me
so hard I had to run, shoulder my back
pack like a driven donkey
as this man dragged me down
the street shouting shouting and with moments
to spare, breathing hard, both of us,
shoved me on a bus, nodding,
smiling widely. My heart panted;
my fingers fumbled for foreign change.
Some passengers clapped. The driver tipped his hat.
Dobrá práce! Gratulujeme!

And over there in a patterned headscarf sat a sloe-eyed old woman giving me the narrow once-over, muttering what I much later learnt, with help, was (I think) *Jeden jazyk nie je nikdy dost* (I think) meaning (I think) *one language is never enough*. It could be I was wrong, again, and she was cursing her husband or god or the book man or me, cursing me, for the delay or just worrying to herself about her sick dog.

And what the book man wanted —
mopping his face with a florid
paisley kerchief; what he asked of me,
making a small circle with the thumb
and forefinger of his right hand,
a shadow rabbit on an absent wall —
was *Mandela Mandela!* A freedom
money with Mandela's head.

He kissed the coin a frenzy,
beamed as the bus pulled away.
Waved. He looked after me
as if we'd known each other
a   long   long   time.

I think of him. How in a second
at the drop of not even a hat

or a hint, he read me pat,

dropped his guard, his book

stall vacant at the station—
(all those titles I could never read)

to run me away with me into my unknown
for a little Mandela. I think of him.

How nothing stays the same,
because life is constant change

and how, unlike in books, there is no
easily going backwards only forwards,

and how difficult that can sometimes be
when all my English is still only English.

Acknowledgements

Versions of some poems have previously been published in fora such as *New Coin, Aerodrome*, the AVBOB competition website, *Five Points, Stanzas*, and the McGregor Poetry Festival Anthologies, or as accompaniment to the Flatfoot Dance Company's performance, *Premonitions*.

Several poems creatively incorporate material from found sources:

'Empathy': http://www.nytimes.com/2009/03/17/science/17prof.html

'Darwin's Deliberations': The Darwin Correspondence Project, manuscript in Cambridge University Library DAR 210.8:2 https://www. darwinproject.ac.uk/tags/about-darwin/family-life/darwin-marriage

'Incredible But True! Phoenomenon': Sadiah Qureshi 'Displaying Sara Baartman, the "Hottentot Venus",' *History of Science* 42, no. 2 (2004): 233–257; and Zoë Strother 'Display of the Body Hottentot' in *Africans on Stage*, edited by Bernth Lindfors (Bloomington, 1999), 1–61.

'Also in 1948': http://www.the-tls.co.uk/articles/public/losing-their-minds/

'Mine and Others': 'Marikana: The Fate of the Families', supplement to the *Mail & Guardian* August 16–22, 2013.

'Re: Reading and Re-reading. Page Proofs': http://www.telegraph.co.uk/women/politics/donald-trump-sexism-tracker-every-offensive-comment-in-one-place/

OTHER WORKS IN THE DRYAD PRESS LIVING POETS SERIES

AVAILABLE NOW

Landscapes of Light and Loss, Stephen Symons
An Unobtrusive Vice, Tony Ullyatt
A Private Audience, Beverly Rycroft
Metaphysical Balm, Michèle Betty

FORTHCOMING IN 2019

happier were the victims, Kambani Ramano
Allegories of the Everyday, Brian Walter

OTHER WORKS BY DRYAD PRESS (PTY) LTD

Unearthed: A selection of the best poems of 2016, edited by
Joan Hambidge and Michèle Betty
The Coroner's Wife: Poems in Translation, Joan Hambidge

Available in South Africa from better bookstores, internationally
from African Books Collective (www.africanbookscollective.com)
and online at www.dryadpress.co.za

DRYAD PRESS
People! Read Poetry

Printed in the United States
By Bookmasters